This book belongs to:

____

Made in the USA
San Bernardino, CA
12 December 2019

61273052R00062